You're Wrong:

Trans Polemics

It's humiliating, really, that i have spent my time on this, in the middle of a pandemic, in the middle of an antiracist uprising.

If the genre of our moment is dystopian science fiction, this is the part before the story begins. This is briefly described in the text that scrolls up the screen at the start of the movie: It's 2020 and a famous children's book author wrote some glib tweets about biology and womanhood, and then when criticized wrote an essay on the danger inherent in trans people being able to access medical treatment. Ok, i told you, minor. Stupid. But here i go.

You've Been Canceled? Wow That's Rough.

I hear you say you did not attack anyone. i believe that you believe that. i believe you believe you are making reasonable, neutral observations, and that you're hurt, and you feel the attacks against you are unfair.

I could point out how entirely canceled and platformless and ostracized and shamed trans people are, every day, in every nation, merely for looking the way they look, for being unable to inhabit a body other than the one they inhabit. Canceled before the season begins. This happens because they are trans, which i know you are suspicious of as an error or a choice. But whether we are trans out of biological imperative or confusion or obstinacy or whatever else you think the reason is, we are trans and we are denied platforms the size of yours because of who we are, and not in fact for attacking anyone else at all.

I hear you say you did not attack anyone, either. (I hear it in my brain like a bell, because the white-woman-who-has-overcome-adversity-and-steeled-herself-against-enemies-of-her-success is familiar to me, as is the gender critical feminist.) So, let's look at the discourse.

You keep saying that you're not transphobic. You mention your one trans friend, in your essay. I believe that you would prefer to not be called a TERF. And i believe that you are hurt by the way people are talking to you, about you. I wonder, then, why you keep saying TERF things, and why each statement is more hurtful than the one before it. I wonder about the history of your views, and whether being attacked has radicalized you, an anti-cancel-culture culture of defensiveness.

Did you respond to adversity by shoring up your position.

Or was it never a mistake.

Your Earnest, Reasonable Concerns

In your tripling-down volley of transphobic tweets, you write "many health professionals are concerned that young people struggling with their mental health are being shunted towards hormones and surgery when this may not be in their best interests," with specific concern for the "lifelong path of medicalization that may result in the loss of their fertility and/or sexual function." You keep rejecting the idea that you are transphobic. You just have this small, soft-spoken, reasonable concern, a question you are innocently asking. You're like my parents in this respect, not transphobic, oh no, just concerned for my health, concerned about changes that are artificial and permanent.

So why do people transition young? Just renegade doctors shunting them off to trans treatment because other mental health interventions seem too hard? No, actually. Many people who transition young do it because they know, young. My last girlfriend's first memory was of wishing there was something like her toy remote control, that could change your gender like changing a channel. I know a trans man who started to pee standing up when he was three. Some of us know, deeply, gnostically, that our bodies have a journey to go on. Other people don't have that gift of certainty, but have some early sense, a nudge, and for us, it is possible that puberty blockers or low dose hormone replacement could help us gather information and buy time.

You say, in a single flippant aside, that the reason people give for allowing youth to transition early is that otherwise they'll kill themselves. I actually think that's a good reason, and worth more than the ten words or so you spend on it. But there is another reason, also.

The longer you have your endogenous hormones cooking, unchecked, in your adolescent and young adult body, the more you will develop secondary sex characteristics caused by those hormones. It is distressing, sure, dysphoria-wise. Even traumatic. For some, perhaps enough to make a person kill themselves. But setting that discomfort aside, going through puberty as one gender can keep you from passing as another gender, later in life. The hormonal cues, (activating hair follicles, thickening bones, redistributing fat,) are things which can only sometimes, and with access, be revised. Then that lack of passability becomes an argument against you, becomes a way to call you a dyke, a man in a dress, a fetishist. It physically prevents trans people from complying with your rules, even if we want to. Even if all we wanted was to go out and be good binary-gendered citizens, posing no threat, no "erosion of womanhood."

If i take you at your word, that you think some trans people are real, but you have concerns associated with gender confirming medical interventions being too easy to access, then i assume that you are calling for more regulation. More restriction. More gatekeeping. More rules. You are operating with a trust that a system that does more to regulate access to trans healthcare will do so safely and fairly. I am surprised that someone who is female bodied and formerly working class has those beliefs, about the medical-insurance-industrial complex, but if you say so, ok. You want more rules, and you think the execution of those rules will be just. You're wrong.

Cis people mostly don't understand what medical transition can consist of and i do not want to pretend to an educator's role about the several types of surgery (chest, genital, face, body sculpting) which may be necessary in a medical transition, nor the distinction between these surgeries and hormone replacement, or what the sequence is likely to be. I trust, since you seem comfortable referring to your own expertise, that you know all that anyway.

I will nonetheless point out that the impact of hormone replacement alone, in particular, allows trans men to pass pretty easily, even if they start quite late. We might be short men with small feet and hands, but the countervailing evidence of facial hair, a broadening jaw, and vocal timbre plus a flannel shirt or whatever does a lot to make us legible as men to causal observers. This is not true of trans women, and this is one of the ways in which they are more vulnerable.

Trans women who take hormones have some effects, (softening skin, fat redistribution,) but these cues, in people who still grow facial hair and have broad jaws and shoulders, are not sufficient to convey "woman" to a lay cis person. They move into a "monster gender" category, an ambiguity that is deeply threatening to cis social structures.

For some trans people, this is in fact the true expression of themselves. Personally, i find this kind of body, the undeniably trans body, to be the most beautiful and powerful of all. But the fact that it is my delight, and that it is a truth for some trans people, does not mean that trans women who want to be interpreted as women by cis people, or who want to adhere to a cis beauty standard, or who want to be less subjected to the violence that comes with that visibility, should be forced into this ambiguous presentation. The trans women that you are likely the most comfortable with are ones who had early or exceptionally well-resourced access to medical interventions.

You say a few times that you think trans people have other mental health concerns, which is a dick move on your part. Yes, we have mental health concerns, as marginalized and traumatized persons often do. That's a real chicken-and-egg situation for you, though. You point specifically to autism and its prevalence in young trans men.

You are concerned about our confusion. Again, i believe that you think you're being helpful. Perhaps some people end up transitioning in ways that later, they will want to rescind, but i don't think that is a tragedy. What is a tragedy is the fact that there are legions of trans people in trapped utter denial or blind terror about coming out, even to themselves. You aren't making a useful point, for people in these positions; by airing your "reasonable" concerns, you are reinforcing their self-loathing, their belief that who they truly are can never be brought into the world.

Some people perhaps transition in the spirit of experimentation, or without total confidence. But even if fluidity or uncertainty gets collapsed, in anti-trans arguments, into some kind of "choice," surely it is still their choice; it is no one else's choice.

You have some specific concerns about medicalization, and also get into the psychiatric vocabulary which, i would argue, is not the language of identity. But, because we rely on the idea of a pathology in order to receive "treatment," trans people often end up facing this diagnostic language. The idea of the "social contagion" of transgenderism, or transgenderism being in the "symptom pool" as you say, does not alarm me, as it alarms you. Yes, more people transition because more people understand that transition is possible. Yes, transition can be in itself a psychologically stressful process, but that is not a reason to try to stop it.

If we're going to use the language of mental illness, although it is a violent system, let me meet you there. "Symptom pools" exist, and do not indicate that the conditions referred to are somehow imaginary. People live in the ways that they know to live, and they go mad in the ways that they know to go mad. Hysterical paralysis, now almost nonexistent, was once a common psychiatric ailment. There was a time when self-cutting was unheard of, an activity only seen in psychosis, and now that type of self-harm is fairly common, and definitely in our cultural consciousness. The thing about transgenderism, even if you frame it as a pathology, is that there is a treatment, as opposed to hysteria or vapours. There is a path forward, and while it may not guarantee happiness (as nothing can, not everyone is capable of happiness) it does contain a possibility of freedom for some people. At least the success rate of "treatment" for trans people is better than the leeches or cocaine or lifelong institutionalization applied to lunatics of the past.

A final point, about how reasonable you think you are being: You talk about how people have reached out to you, backchannel, to say that they are relieved to hear your opinion. You say this as though it is proof that you're outspoken, brave, correct. Ma'am, your platform is one of the largest of any private citizen on earth. If you espoused anything, no matter how abhorrent, do you think there would not be people coming to you with thanks? If you were championing gay conversion therapy, if you advocated for eugenics based on racial phrenology, you would still get people in your DMs agreeing, so grateful to you, for speaking up.

The Idea That Anyone Has One Fixed Gender Over Their Life Course Is Absurd

Listen, it is a lie. It's a lie that there is a gender binary that works for most people, and then there are some people who need to go from one polarity to the other, and then there are some people who occupy a third nonbinary location. Every human being is selecting and constructing their gender not from a binary, but from an infinite range. We do this every day, every hour, of our lives.

I was told i'll need to substantiate this claim. LOL. I could try to refer you to other writers defending this position, but the reason i know this is not because of other writers, it's because i am alive in a body and i am paying attention. Other people of course give me freedom (and inspiration, through their example, through their survival.) But the information itself is inside us, inside every person. We have been sold a fiction of immutable, binary, biological sex, and a further fiction of gender roles and power hierarchies that emerge from that system.

Think about what gender is. Then think about whether Amber Rose and Tina Fey are "the same gender." Think about who you were when you were nine, or twelve, or sixteen, and who you are now, and ask yourself if your gender was the same.

The reality that some people detransition is used (by you, for example) to delegitimize trans identity, when in fact it argues for the need for a destruction of the conception of gender that we live under more clearly than anything. You seem to be concerned with young assigned-female people losing their ability to have children in the conventional way. This seems to replicate what the "demeaning" reduction of womanhood to reproductive capacity which you decry, when you think someone is calling you a "menstruator," but setting that aside i think you misunderstand detransition.

Detransitioners are not uniform, their experience is not the same. Some move into another phase of transition because the feelings that initially guided them guide them somewhere else. Many are faced with the reality of transphobia, familial rejection, and the difficulty of passing (or accessing adequate medical interventions they would need in order to pass) and then try to return to the painful relative safety of living in their former lives. Neither outcome indicates, to me, that transition (or access to medical technology that facilitates transition) is a problem.

Gender is not so different from style. (I am trying to not make this a thing with references, but this isn't my independent idea—Judith Butler and Eve Kosofsky Sedgwick have written extensively on this.) It is, or it should be, trivial.

It is only not trivial because people die for it, are killed for it. People are not upset with you for being glib or ignorant or even insulting, though you have been all those things. People are upset with you because when someone with your enormous platform asserts that trans women are not real women because they don't menstruate, there is a connection between rhetoric and violence. In the week that i have been writing this to you, six Black trans women have been murdered in America.

And to say that what should be preserved, in the face of murder over the failure to perform gender "correctly," is the validity of womanhood, the sovereignty of biological sex, is tantamount to blaming victims for their own murder.

Differences in Violence
Although you expend a lot of your mental energy on how and why men like me should reconsider existing, the truth is that your use of your platform is more damaging to trans women. Trans women are more vulnerable than trans men, trans women of color especially. Six Black trans women have been murdered since i've been writing this, to you.

Why? Why does the Anti Violence Project reliably find, in its annual data collection, that trans women are (by an order of magnitude) more likely to experience violence, including fatal violence, than other kinds of trans people?

In her interview in Disclosure, Jen Richards says that men who've had sex with trans women suddenly fear ridicule from their friend group, for having sex with a quote-unquote man. I don't think that's it. I don't think it is a fear of ridicule or social censure, i think that the men who kill trans women are afraid of something within themselves.

Through sex we know each other. Maybe, in distant historical periods, we knew each other through community, through shared spaces and social ties, through family. All of that has eroded, and now we increasingly know each other most deeply through sex, and that depth is shallow too. We can't admit how we need each other and become each other and see inside of each other, during sex. The vulnerability is intolerable.

So, we try to stick with the story on the surface, a physiological act, and we try to make that story even simpler. We conflate sex and power and subservience. Capitalism is a conspirator in this as well, introducing the false premise that the thing that we want, when we want sex (which, again, is being deeply seen and accepted and known in a way that is not available to us in normal, non-erotically charged encounters) belongs to the affluent, or can be bought.

In a conventional model, a man penetrates, colonizes, owns, defiles. And the woman, the bottom, is the defiled, the field, the hole, the object that is destroyed by use.

If that is how we understand ourselves, in sex, the violence directed at trans and queer bodies becomes easy to understand. We threaten a system of power and control which is how heterosexuals navigate the world. This is also tied to American individualism and capitalist ethos; the belief that what happens to you does not impact me; i can destroy someone else without destroying myself. By this logic i can even profit from that destruction, without consequence.

Focusing specifically on violence against trans women, trans women are harmed and killed because of what male-to-female transgenderism implies, for the heteropatriarchal power structure. By the logic that needs to understand sex as an exchange of power, a trans man or a butch lesbian does not threaten the power structure itself. Someone who was subjugated and wants to be a subjugator, within rape culture, does not necessarily pose a threat, so long as there is enough complicity once they switch camps. Also, to be blunt, a trans man or butch lesbian can be raped, as a heterosexual corrective.

But trans women, (amalgamated in the transphobe's mind with bottoms, drag queens, effeminate men,) trans women annihilate the whole carceral system of gender, by moving out of the power which, by biological right, should be theirs. They cannot be forced into being men, and rape cannot repair them. Transphobes understand this as a choice, an abdication. The threat inherent in the possibility that a man can surrender his manhood is unbearable.

Maybe, when the sex partners of trans women kill trans women, they are terrified of how they have seen themselves mirrored in the sex act they've completed. Maybe they are viscerally disgusted by the thing that they desired, moments before. I don't know. But it doesn't happen to trans men at the same frequency or scale.

I spend most of my imaginary argument with you talking about Society, but there is one thing i can say, about violence in my own life. (I have of course been raped since my transition. I was also once pushed down a flight of stairs, which broke my arm. People i tried to love made it their project to tell me that my sexuality was disgusting. Plenty of things have happened. But i want to make a more specific point.)

When i started taking testosterone, catcalling and the bravado-performance element of hetero flirtation fell away quickly. That was a relief, although at the same time small privileges which i had not noticed, little niceties and considerations people (mostly men) had once given me also vanished.

What came in its place, for those first few months, was a secret, silent, driven attention from individual men. It happened every week or two. They followed me home, they masturbated at me on the subway, they urinated while staring at me on the street. They did this without anyone else knowing, without their boys yelling encouragement or any witness for me to roll my eyes at. Underneath these gestures, instead of the hetero men's catcalling message—I'd be so great at having sex with you! Why don't you appreciate me telling you that! – was the certainty that these men wanted to murder me. It was sexual attention, yes, but the sexuality was incidental to a private threat of violence. It happened for about five months, (i kept a journal.) Then it stopped happening. I don't know why, although it is possible that those men thought i was a trans woman, at the time, when i was a little softer. It's a mistake some people still make.

Your "Deep Empathy"
I don't want to do what you did, and weaponize my history of being assaulted to legitimize my argument. I'd rather not. But you have somewhat forced my hand, by claiming that your experience of domestic violence gives you a proximity, a "deep empathy," towards what murdered trans women feel in their last moments. If you had that empathy, it still would not excuse or justify the things you've said. But you do not have that empathy.

I don't have it either.

Because even in my bloodiest and most terrified moments with Bad Lovers, (in the worst that i've survived) (when i knew i would not survive) (when i betrayed my own frantic misery with the desire for survival) i did not know what it meant, what it means, to be a non-passing trans woman. Neither of us know what it is to live in a world that relentlessly—listen to me, every moment—focuses its derision and hostility on you. The hypervigilance, the adrenal fatigue, the knowledge that violence could come from anywhere at any time. The knowledge that when violence comes, there will be plenty of people who think that being who you are is enough reason to justify whatever was done to you. I don't know (neither do you) what it is to live like that and then find someone who seems to offer some closeness, a possibility of being seen, and then have that person become, instead, the instrument of your death.

Of course, it isn't only intimates of trans women who kill trans women. Strangers, acquaintances, police officers, fathers, classmates, the list is long and various. Which is how you can tell that one of the factors is a culture of devaluation, objectification, and violence towards trans women. Which is how someone other than yourself might have decided, instead, that saying flippant things about the illegitimacy or suspiciousness of trans identities is not the neutral, reasonable observation of a thoughtful person at this time.

Aren't They All Prostitutes
I'm in rural North Carolina in the kitchen of a run-down farmhouse. Me and three other volunteers are languidly cleaning up after dinner, a bunch of sweet liberals. Another volunteer, a European soft boy, wants to have a conversation about the dream charities we would all start. This girl has

just passionately talked about water conservation. It's my turn. I say, "Well, something for Black trans women. A fund, i guess." The boy says "Well, ok, but why Black trans women?" meaning, if i'm going to make something why exclude myself, people like myself.

I say, "Because it's harder for them, and it's because of work that they do that it's safe for me to be who i am."

"It's harder for them?"

"Yeah, in terms of discrimination and violence. It's harder for them to make money. I mean, people kill them."

He says, "Doesn't that happen because they're prostitutes?" and the air breaks inside of the room, my brain flickering.

I say, "Even if that's true why do you think they end up being prostitutes?" and he hems and haws and walks it back.

Justice for trans people is largely about addressing poverty, addressing access to resources, work, opportunities, and networks of support that have historically been denied to us. Denied to us in part because of reasonable concerns from reasonable people in power, such as yourself. There is a problem of opportunity, i don't want to undersell that.

I don't want to romanticize this, because i know many trans people, (many sex workers of all genders) are pushed into the sex trades because of necessity and survival and circumstance, and are not happy there. It's a field i've been in, yes, and also that there are kinds of hustle within the industry that i haven't had to do. I don't want to represent myself as an expert.

But still i feel compelled to say that sex work is not something to apologize for. It is work that finds us because of what cis people think of us, which is not something that we should be ashamed of. And the special ability of trans people as sex workers, apart from our carnal and technical abilities, not just for our knowledge of the Other Body and its needs, but for our holiness, our mysticism, our ability to take in the parts of men that men will forever deny. This is not a coincidence or, necessarily, a tragedy. It is part of our gift to the world. And like many of our gifts, the cost to us is sometimes dear.

My Sexual Obsession is Problematic

Plenty of people, including some trans thought leaders who i actually care about, would say that my focus on the sex is counterproductive. The representation of trans people as sexual, sexualized entities, and the sexual trans body as the site where knowledge originates, is counterproductive. Like cis people, we do not have to be our bodies, it is not our only story. So, my focus is problematic. Yes i know.

Then why the emphasis?

Because as someone who presented as a Strange Girl and then as an illegible creature and then as, (i'm guessing, i honestly couldn't say for sure) an effeminate man, sex has been forefronted whether i wanted it to be or not, in most of the interactions i have had since i was about twelve years old.

I've been thinking and writing about sexual violence (often quite badly!) since i was fourteen.

My sex obsession is me trying to put my Malcom-Gladwell-genius-10k-mastery-hours to use.

This is one of the areas where i look forward to the extinction of my own cohort. I'm not into respectability politics for myself (that ship has sailed anyway,) but when i talk to young trans people, who have grown up seeing trans people who are not sex monsters in the media around them, what they know about the validity and possibility of their lives is something i never knew. It is an endless sweetness, to me, to be in the generation which witnesses this shift.

And that shift is something you would deny them. You have denied them.

The Desire for Bad Language

Here's a hot, potentially irresponsible, take; non-binary is a shitty word for it. Because it implies that there is a binary, rather than a spectrum. Because it implies that binary gender, men and women, are real and that the construct of men and women is not, in itself, deeply wounding even to the vast majority of those who are cis and perform their gender "correctly." The whole thing is poison. The whole thing is a system of stereotyping, othering, oppression, repression and control. In that respect, in the respect that i want the entire system to be destroyed, i suppose i am advocating for the "erosion of biological sex" or the "erasure of womanhood."

Mykki Blanco (genius, heroine) talks about not identifying with they/them pronouns, which often get used for her as an attempt at deference or inclusion. She says that, growing up, she and the people she ran with were cunts. I love the word cunt too.

Fucked up language is very satisfying. You don't like being called a bitch but i detect a little hubris and self-satisfaction when you call yourself a bitch. In close company, i call myself "a tran" or "a transgender," even "transsexual," even the porno abbreviation TS. The first image of a trans person i saw was an ad for fetish phone sex snuck in the back of one of my father's hetero porn magazines. It was a small black-and-white photo in a black-bounded rectangle with a phone number. The language in the ad copy was not polite. She was wearing lingerie. This was the only visual reference i had for a trans person until i was in my early 20s. This is the language i grew up with, the language that was used to try to warn me to not be who i am. It's oppositional, and dated, and not progressive, but i am so into it.

I think this is the same impulse that makes me want to disgust you with my body. The desire to make something cruel and pyrotechnic, a knot in straight consciousness, a sign pointing to the fissure in the land you're all claiming is solid ground.

This is a problem overarching this project. I am kind of trying to explain it to you, the connection between your speech and the chronic violence we face. And explanation is futile. You won't read this, not even if someone puts it in your hand. No one is convinced out of bigotry by argument. Because bigotry isn't a lack of information; it is, as Du Bois wrote of racism, a vicious habit of mind. But since you use the rhetoric of convincing people of your rightness i am falling into a rhetoric-of-convincing as well. And that prevents me from making this beautiful. Beauty and truth are not interchangeable, and i would rather have beauty. I would rather have the diamonds in my blood which are part of a queer ancestry, i would rather have a hole that men pay to lick before going home to their pretty cis wives, i'd rather be the nightmare buffalo bill in a kimono touching his nipples, a queer-coded villain, i'd rather be problematic. It's more fun and i'm better at it. But then i have to worry what the straights will think of The Community (LOL) based on my sloppy language. I resent you for that.

It's not benign, either, the constant need to explain and justify our existence to cis people. It makes us stupider. It forces us into a reductive position, because it seems more defensible. It forces us to make nosological categories, labels, based not on ourselves but on the comfort and literacy of cis people.

Then we look for ourselves inside of the basic descriptions we crafted to try to convince cis people that we exist, and of course we end up dissatisfied.

But we can't say we're dissatisfied, we can't say we're yet another other thing, straining beyond language, because that makes us too difficult. We can't name any discomfort or malaise, in fact, without it being used as a point of ridicule to say transition isn't real, we should not have transitioned in the first place. Imagine believing that your identity had to make you happy, in order for it to be "real."

Womban
Explaining the inciting incident of this abuse of your twitter-powers, you say several times that the language "people who menstruate" is demeaning, a demeaning substitute for the word woman. I know that a lot of people have pointed out to you, with varying degrees of politeness, that this ignores not just trans people (including men who menstruate, such as myself) but also cis women who do not

menstruate. It's really a lot of people to insult and then insist upon insulting.

Your preoccupation here, with the idea that being a "menstruator" is degrading, doesn't bear scrutiny. If being a woman should not be about menstruation, because that conflation is demeaning, doesn't it follow that trans women should be welcomed as examples of womanhood not tethered to a humiliating biology?

This kind of logic is rampant in an underbelly of the internet that i can't really fathom. I know you do not want to be labeled as a gender critical feminist or TERF or whatever, but menstruation is one of their favorite subjects. It's not simply that trans women are somehow threatening or repulsive, there seems to be a need, among people with this ideology, to be aggressive and disrespectful and actively point it out to as many trans women as possible. This in turn leads to online behavior from cis women the likes of which i have never seen. Cis women tweeting at strangers about their "delicious succulent natural vaginas," for example. And massive amounts of discourse on menstruation and childbirth and their "horrors," which trans people (according to you) can't fathom.

The argument i suppose being that if the trans woman could produce some proof of adequate suffering she could graduate into womanhood.

Again, i would argue that trans women suffer for womanhood more than anyone. I would argue that trans people know about horror and the body.

Differences in Violence: Representation and History

Like the preoccupation with gender, when gender is mostly gesture and style, it would be nice if the concern about "representation" were trivial, but it is not. Cultural production is important. We understand what a society values by looking at its artifacts.

They gave us enough TV shows that we are at a cultural tipping point, it's so stupid. The western-media-consuming-mind is the dumbest. Like a little transparent blobfish. They put trans people on television thinking we would exist as a fetish, ornament, virtue signal of the producers' tolerance and progressive values. And then we began to tell our own stories.

Because we've reached this critical mass of trans representation and are having a weird trend moment, a lot of cis people seem to be under the impression that trans people are new.

Trans people have existed since people have existed. And the cis need for trans people has existed for a long time too. The cis need for trans people is the need to subjugate the body, deny the sex drive, sanitize and gatekeep the idea of masculinity as the seat of power.

How long has it been. Focusing on "Western" culture, some thinkers pin the emergence of split between the mind-soul and body (and therefore, the assessment of the body as un-valuable, dirty, dangerous) to the Hellenic period in Greece.

I have heard some spiritual teachers trace the problem earlier, to the advent of agriculture. In a pre-agricultural society (which had plenty of brutality and problems of its own) people were in constant communication with each other and with the land, in order to survive. We were interdependent. The communities were small, and the connections deep. You relied on your environment. Then, as agriculture emerged and land became something you could own, nature something you could protect yourself from, other problems of ownership arose. Who owns whom. To whom does the family "belong." A need for role rigidity and subjugation emerged.

Whether you trace the need for gender policing to Ancient Greece or to the shift to agrarian society, once the need for subjugation arose, trans people (and other "othered" bodies—queers, enslaved people, women,) became receptacles for the terror and desire of the people who had power over them.

We do this shadow work for "normal" people all the time, whether it is conscious or not, whether we consent to it or not.

The way that gender functions in society (and the way society functions, as a consequence) is seismically shifting. I know you hate it. Can it be stopped? Can you be successful, in your attempt to recloset, detransition, delegitimize the trans people you attack under the guise of earnest thoughtful feminist questioning.

I hope not, but i think that a kind of backward movement is possible, yes. I think we could be erased as agents of our own stories, turned back into some pervert menace or a bunch of confused children. You could erase our ability to be human in the general consciousness, but you could never erase the image of the tranny from the "normal" men's sexual imagination. Sexually depraved, hermaphroditical, chimerical, insatiable, best of all the worlds at once. We exist as an ur-fantasy on a substrate of cis erotic consciousness, a reservoir of disgust, a lightning rod for possibility. Ultimately you cannot erase us because we are part of you. You need us too badly.

Yes, we are in a moment where the attitude and social consciousness towards trans people is revolutionizing. Revolutions create problems too, which is one reason (aside from the secret hope that oppression will continue forever,) that institutions are so invested in selling us on incremental change. Incremental change is less disruptive, less harmful, by a logic that is willing to ignore the harm inherent in preserving a status quo.

If this is a moment of revolution, what are you and the other gender critical types on the internet trying to accomplish. If this is revolution, what comes after revolutions. If this is freedom, what is the reconstruction.

I Think You Should Read Conflict is Not Abuse
It's a good book. A brief, and oversimplified version of my understanding is this:

Schulman traces a pattern of thought and behavior from its smallest manifestation, playing out in a flirtation, to larger and larger arenas, ultimately talking about Palestine.

The cycle she describes, roughly, is that people who are fragile and have a low distress tolerance, when they feel hurt, assume that they have been willfully harmed (abused) by someone, to cause them to feel that way. This reactive fragility can come from two separate tracks, two different personalities: people who have been traumatized, who are thrown into reexperiencing their trauma by being hurt, and people who come from a background of entitlement and are so unaccustomed to facing any form of challenge or struggle that discomfort of any kind is experienced as an attack.

I think you should read Conflict is Not Abuse and then think about why it is that you are so upset by the idea of the "erosion" of biological sex.

Is it because that admission, that biological sex and gender are not innately connected, would force you to acknowledge that other people are more oppressed than you, a woman?

Are you afraid of losing your righteousness. Of being dethroned.

Transmasculine Grievance
Even though i'm talking a lot about how if you want to criticize trans people or identities, you should perhaps shut up (or journal about it, whisper it into a seashell, whatever, something other than tell your fourteen million twitter fans) i am going to talk a little about a criticism i have of trans people. I'm going to talk about transmasculine grievance.

This happens on twitter and reddit. I think the people who do it are young trans men who don't have a lot of tools or opportunities for self-reflection. Basically, trans men periodically get mad that trans women get more attention.

And trans women do get more attention, because they get murdered more, and so they fight for their lives more.

Trans women do more movement and organizing work. They create community in part because they rely more on community, being so thoroughly discriminated against in terms of employment and other formal modes of support. They do this while also facing more violence and overt discrimination than trans men.

Trans men, sure, sometimes get traumatized and have a hard time. But we also get tenure track professorships and write articles for New Inquiry and provide an edgy table dressing of queerness for organizations that would not allow what they imagine is the instability and sexualization that a trans woman would foment in their midst.

I say this partly to own that i am, with my caucacity and my master's degree, imperfect as a messenger. I am for example given to licking my own wounds and arguing with authors when my time could be better spent.

I say this also to point out that some trans people will stand with you. Which you will also interpret as proof of your correctness and progressivism. My point is that we are capable of betraying our sisters. In fact, we do it all the time.

Laws

Just like you have one trans friend, i have one anti-cancel culture friend. Look how open minded we both are. It's his fault i'm doing this, actually. He told me people were upset at your essay for no reason. "It's not that bad," he said. (My contention is that it is that bad, if you couldn't tell. The fact that someone could think it's not that bad is part of what makes it so bad.)

My friend says "i just think women should have a right to a penisless bathroom." He says "they shut down this battered women's shelter because they wouldn't take trans women." He wants to talk about prisons. Gendered spaces. I say that early transition and androgynous trans women are not safe in men's spaces, and he says "i believe that," but there's no solution.

"i just think women should have a right to a penisless bathroom" is something i can imagine you saying. The same framing of a "reasonable concern" about the problems created by trans people.

This logic has so many problems it's hard to deal with it at all. It's a feeling i had reading your essay, which i also have when i read Dworkin, (whose prose style and passion i find really enviable,) as though i am in a childhood house in a dream wrestling a jello octopus; my hand goes through what it tries to grab onto. I think i've escaped and the floor falls away. I cannot argue to satisfaction with someone whose premise is that i should not exist. But i guess that's what i am trying to do, here, so. Ok. A rule that centers on a penis as a threat of harm only serves to entrench that ideology, and the associated also incorrect ideology that people without penises are incapable of harm. The center of a Venn diagram of people who will perpetrate sexual violence in a bathroom and people who will only go into a bathroom if they have a legally protected right to occupy that bathroom based on their sex is, i imagine, very small. Perpetration of sexual violence by trans people is very very very very rare; Based on the amount of trauma we are forced to absorb, it is a testament to us that we do not hurt others more often. I could go on.

Putting aside the numerous problems with using the specter of a predator in a bathroom to legislate about gendered spaces, there is another problem with the trans bathroom discourse, which is that you cannot eradicate sexual violence by the creation of more robust laws. If someone manages to not rape or murder other people in their community because they fear the severity of the punishment, they'll face, society has already failed itself by creating that person.

I'm not a lawyer or legal scholar, i don't feel equipped to say what the law should do, but it's clear that the law fails us when it comes to gender, sex, bodily autonomy, questions that are by their nature partly internal, gradated, fluctuating. I could never have proved that i was trans before i took hormones for a couple years and grew my fourteen little chin hairs.

One problem with looking to a law to create justice, is that it presumes that justice is possible. In fact, there is no justice, in the wake of real wrongdoing. The man who hurt me for several years, starting when i was fifteen, could not give me restitution that would allow me to be the person i could have been, if that had not happened. I often wish that this man would pay me, (a lot of his exploitation of me was financial.) But even if he gave me a bunch of money, i wouldn't be ok.

If he were locked up, it would just be him and his daddy issues, even more rageful for being locked up. It would not help me. I don't think that there is any hope for him.

He'll die being who he is.

I know what you're wondering now. When "gender critical" types learn that i'm also a survivor, they have the same question. "Do you think you are the way you are because of what happened to you." A reasonable question like all your reasonable questions. The question is, of course, transphobic. The presumption that our identity comes from being damaged in some way is offensive. And forcing us to choose between admitting we've been hurt and having an identity that's legitimate is cruel.

I'll be honest with you, though, since you've come this far with me.

I don't know who i would be without my trauma. I don't think that can be known.

What i know is that the thing which changed inside my body, which needed to be seen and treated differently, is the best of me. That part of me is my gift. If i only get it because i was raped (and raped, and raped) then that is a price i paid in order to become this person. So i can't let you tell people to be afraid of it, to reject the "symptom pool," to distrust what their body tells them. I can't be silent while you say that.

Why I'm Still Writing This

I don't know, girl. Honestly, it's a sickness.

You talk a lot about people calling you names, about the resistance you've faced, how easily and fully and floridly people moved to cancel you. You talk about it i assume because it was hurtful, and also because you believe it is clearly unfair. You want to solidify your position as a Brave Woman Speaking Out.

i won't call you names, though i do sometimes wish that you could be emotionally hurt, in the way that you have hurt so many people i care about, a sort of vengeance.

I wish, in fact, that you could see my body, because i assume you would find it repulsive, and i admit to taking a perverse pleasure in that. It's a theme in my own work, (the creative work i do when i'm not stupidly dragged into writing imaginary 30-page letters,) inflicting my horrible body on an audience.

The last girl i loved, at the end, was disgusted by my body. (And when i say i loved her, i mean her little dinosaur walk, her bright strange eyes, her hatchling eggshell crooked tooth, her sparkly puzzlebox brain—she was everything at once, fierce and tender and bold and shy. My galaxy twin.) She was repulsed by me not because i'm trans but because she is not attracted to men. She thought she might have been able to work it out for me, because i had some other good qualities, and also a vagina, but finally it was insurmountable.

She is trans too. Part of why she doesn't love men is that, before she was fifteen, her stepfather had visited unspeakable violence onto her body, (because she was trans? Or would he have done that to any child? He had trans pornos in the house too. I think he knew.) He hurt her, as a child, enough for a lifetime. Enough to keep her from coming out until after she was 30, because she knew it wasn't safe. Violence is sticky, you know, once it happens it tends to happen. As an adult, she was beaten almost to death in a men's room (where, i believe, by your logic, she was supposed to be.) This man, who did not know her, broke several bones in her face, one of her eye orbits still thickened and strange from it. It's not the most important thing, about the violence, but it did also keep her from loving me.

Her health insurance does not cover the facial feminization surgery which is part of the alternately too frivolous or too serious gender affirming procedures you are concerned about people having. She wants it, and i think it might really help. She is short and shy and not a good fighter. People might hit her less if she looked like your idea of a girl.

It isn't kind of me, i know, to pimp out her story when i have one of my own. But it is connected, that people like you think she's not a woman because she doesn't look like your idea of a woman, so she shouldn't be protected, she should be suspect, a predator, a threat in the women's room. By the dominant gender critical logic, she should be denied care and support. She should be where she is, scraping by, barely not getting fired from minimum wage work where people call her by her dead name. There is a line, from that circumstance, to the violence, to how she isn't with me. And i don't forgive you for that.

The Internet and How We Talk

I tried again to stop writing this. Then that letter came out, in Harpers, on the importance of "justice and open debate." Then the pr*sident talked about cancel culture in his speech where he bemoaned the tearing down of monuments to slavery. I am having a problem of scale and perspective. Things are flattening. This is probably evident, in that i am talking to a random famous author as though she were a person in my life. In normal times, i'd try to remedy this perspectival loss by getting off the internet, but right now the internet is the only game in town.

As social networking platforms have discovered how to monetize themselves, they prioritize communication less and less. What twitter wants, as a financial entity, is virality and engagement. It is a machine which, sometimes, has been minorly subverted in the hands of the skillful or the desperate. Revolutions, uprisings, have been facilitated by twitter, despite itself. It has, in some ways, democratized information, and has allowed some people who would otherwise have no platform to speak out powerfully. And yet it is still SO BAD.

I don't care that much about you being personally attacked, though i guess it's counterproductive for people to be attacking you, rather than your bad ideas. In a sense it's not your fault that anyone gives a shit what you say. You're just famous, and it's a broader social failing that famous people are now regarded as experts.

Here is where, through a mobius strip of reasoning, i do begin to agree with you. There is a problem in how we talk.

Everything starts to mobius around itself. The "free speech" crew are upset about being attacked and deplatformed, so they end up ouroborosing into a demand for civility. No amount of "civility" will erase the fact that powerful people can now be critiqued when they say fucked up things. Conversely, yes, "cancel culture," or the emotional fragility and empathic failure that makes it impossible for people to continue to be in shared space when there is perceived harm, does exist. Sometimes the outcome may be an improvement. But the overall mechanism, (fragility, intolerance, black-and-white thinking,) is an outcome of the same values that suppose that sufficiently punitive rules will force people into good behavior. It is a culture of fear.

Again, i think you should read Conflict Is Not Abuse. I think you should look at the thinking of the folks who worked on the #8toabolition campaign. Because the call to accountability is a call to remain in communication, to admit that there is some thread of community and mutual reliance which runs through all of us. And that implies, yes, that people should not threaten your life on the internet, just as it implies that you could listen to the ways in which your reasonable speech encouraged violence and discrimination towards a vulnerable group of people and be accountable to that.

The idea of a world without violence, beyond violence, (no cops, no masters, no mean dad gods,) is easy to dismiss as utopian and childish. But it's what we must try to move towards. Nothing else is worth striving for. Any other formulation leaves us with this tyranny somewhere. If it's not her stepfather, it's a children's book author. If it's not president-rapist it's president-other-rapist. It may not feel possible, or realistic, but the change that we need, if we are going to redeem ourselves as a species, is radical in the extreme.

I think there will be a world beyond this violence, if we survive at all. (Big if!) But a precondition of that world is that the people who need to be having this conversation die. We're the dinosaurs, but it's ok. You'll die. And i'll die. I look forward to that.

Who Wrote This
This text is a working document produced by C. Bain for tiresias projekt (tiresiasprojekt.com).

There are ways to help and support trans people. I encourage looking online for individuals who need support (#transcrowdfund and #openyourpurse are tags people use, many people act as aggregators.) I recommend seeking individuals because for those of us with trauma histories taking action to access resources through any organization can become an obstacle, (even asking for direct aid, of course, is an obstacle.) There are organizations that work closely with impacted communities as well, two that come immediately to mind are The Okra Project and Black Trans Travel Fund.